THE DECIDUOUS FOREST BIOME

Colin Grady

Enslow Publishing
101 W. 23rd Street
Suite 240
New York, NY 10011
USA

enslow.com

WORDS TO KNOW

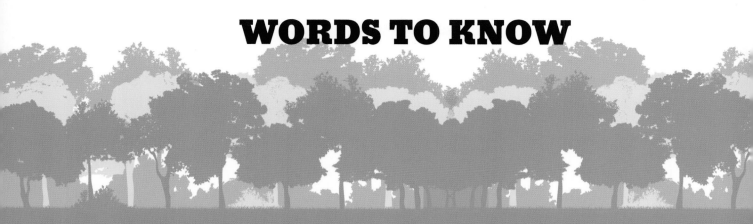

canopy—The highest part of a forest that is made up of the tops of tall trees.

climate—The weather conditions in a place over a period of years.

community—A group of living things that share the same area.

decay—To rot or break down.

herb—Small, soft-stemmed plants that are often used for medicine and food seasoning.

layer—One thickness or level of something that is on top of another.

shrub—A low, bushy plant.

stems—The parts of a plant that hold the leaves.

understory—The layer in a deciduous forest where small animals, plants, and young trees live and grow.

CONTENTS

In the deciduous forest biome, most trees lose their leaves in the fall and grow new ones in the spring.

The Deciduous Forest Biome

A biome is a community of plants and animals that live together in a certain place and climate. There are many different biomes, such as deserts and the ocean. Another kind of biome is the deciduous forest.

What Is a Deciduous Forest?

Deciduous forests are found mainly in North America, Europe, and Asia. These forests have four seasons—winter, spring, summer, and fall. Most of the trees in a deciduous forest lose their leaves in the fall.

The areas in green on the map show where the deciduous forests of the world are found.

When leaves start to die, they lose their green color. They turn red, orange, yellow, and brown until they fall off the tree.

By losing their leaves, the trees in a deciduous forest are able to live through cold winters. If the leaves stayed on the trees in the winter, they would freeze. Icy leaves would weigh the branches down and make the branches snap and break off the trees. In the spring, the trees grow new green leaves.

What Does It Mean?

The word *deciduous* comes from the Latin language and means "to fall off."

The Forest Layers

There are five layers in a deciduous forest: canopy, understory, shrub, herb, and floor. Each layer is an important part of the forest and has different plants and animals living in it.

Canopy

The branches and leaves of the tallest trees make up the canopy. Trees of the canopy receive the most sunlight. Birds that eat fruit live in the canopy. Insects and mammals that eat

The canopy is the top part of the deciduous forest.

leaves or fruit also live in the canopy. Vines grow in the canopy. Flowers and fruit on the vines become food for birds and other animals.

Understory

Young trees, small trees, and plants make up the understory. These trees and plants grow well without much light. They have broad, flat leaves. The leaves help the plants catch the sunlight that is not blocked by the canopy. Some of these plants lose their leaves each year.

The understory has smaller trees and plants.

Useful and Yummy

Many of the trees in the deciduous forest contain sap, a thick, sticky liquid. The sap can protect the tree's roots from freezing during the cold winter months. In the spring, it can be used to make delicious syrup!

Shrub

The shrub layer is home to many birds and insects. Shrubs have woody stems like trees. However, they usually have more than one stem and do not grow as large as trees.

Herb

Ferns, grasses, wildflowers, and very young trees make up the herb layer. Forest

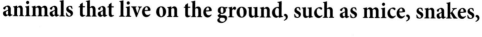

This forest floor is covered by a flowering plant called bear's garlic.

animals that live on the ground, such as mice, snakes,

The forest is full of wildlife like deer and squirrels.

bears, and deer, make their home here.

Floor

The ground of the forest makes up the floor. Low plants, such as moss, can often be found on the forest floor. The floor is also covered by leaves, twigs, and other things that fall from higher layers.

Birds Plant Seeds

Birds in the deciduous forest can help plant new trees. The blue jay lives in the deciduous forest. It takes oak seeds from the forest and drops them onto farm fields. The seeds grow into trees.

Blue jays make their home in the forests of North America.

Soil in the Deciduous Forest

The deciduous forest has very rich soil. This soil makes it easy for new trees and plants to grow. Why is the soil so rich? Believe it or not, it is thanks to dead plants and animals!

Soil and Decay

When an animal dies in the forest, it begins to decay, or rot. When leaves fall to the ground in the fall, they decay also.

A dead tree decomposes in the forest. As it rots, it makes the soil richer.

Other living things, such as worms and spiders, help to break down the plants and animals even more. What is left is good for the soil.

The Useful Forest

The deciduous forest is useful to people in many different ways. They can use the wood from the forest to build their homes. Then they can use more wood to cook and heat their homes. Some wood from deciduous forests is taken to factories, where it is made into paper. Plastics and cloth can also be made from the trees of the deciduous forest.

A man builds a house with wood. People use wood for many different things. We must be sure that there are enough trees left in the forest.

Cutting Down Trees

In order to make paper and other important items, trees must be cut down. People have cut down many trees from deciduous forests. Forests used to cover one half of Earth's surface, but now they only cover one third. We have cut down too many trees. When forests are destroyed, many plants and animals that live there are hurt.

The Importance of Trees

Deciduous forest plants and trees, like all green plants, give off oxygen and add to our air supply. Forests also soak up extra rainwater to prevent floods. Without the forests, many kinds of plants and animals could not live. The deciduous forest biome is important to many forms of life.

The deciduous forest is home to many animals, trees, and plants. We need to take care of this important biome.

ACTIVITY
DRAWING THE FOREST

In this book you learned about the different layers of the deciduous forest. Let's make a picture of what is found in each of the layers.

1. Do some research online to learn more about what kinds of animals live in each layer of the deciduous forest. Write down a few animals for each layer.

2. On a large blank piece of paper, draw a few tall trees. The top of these will represent the canopy.

3. Add some smaller, younger trees to show the understory.

4. Draw some shrubs and smaller plants to represent herbs.

5. Finally, add some soil.

6. Now add a couple of animals for each layer of the forest.

7. Be sure to label each of the five layers, as well as all plants and animals that you have included.

LEARN MORE

Books

Duke, Shirley. *Seasons of the Deciduous Forest Biome*. Vero Beach, FL: Rourke, 2014.

Fleisher, Paul. *Forest Food Webs*. Minneapolis, MN: Lerner, 2013.

Johansson, Philip. *The Temperate Forest: Discover This Wooded Biome*. New York: Enslow, 2015.

Laber-Warren, Emily. *A Walk in the Woods: Into the Field Guide*. New York: Downtown Bookworks, 2013.

Websites

Ducksters
ducksters.com/science/ecosystems/temperate_forest_biome.php
Interesting facts about the temperate forest biome.

Kids Do Ecology
kids.nceas.ucsb.edu/biomes/temperateforest.html
Photos and links to information about the temperate forest

INDEX

Published in 2017 by Enslow Publishing, LLC.
101 W. 23rd Street, Suite 240, New York, NY 10011
Copyright © 2017 by Enslow Publishing, LLC

Library of Congress Cataloging-in-Publication Data
Names: Grady, Colin, author.
Title: The deciduous forest biome / Colin Grady.
Description: New York, NY : Enslow Publishing, 2017. | "2017 | Series: Zoom in on biomes | Audience: Ages 7+ | Audience: Grades 1 to 3. | Includes bibliographical references and index.
Identifiers: LCCN 2015048568| ISBN 9780766077515 (library bound) | ISBN 9780766077485 (pbk.) | ISBN 9780766077492 (6-pack)
Subjects: LCSH: Forest ecology--Juvenile literature. | Forest animals--Juvenile literature. | Forests and forestry--Juvenile literature.
Classification: LCC QH541.5.F6 S875 2017 | DDC 577.3--dc23
LC record available at http://lccn.loc.gov/2015048568

Printed in Malaysia

To Our Readers: We have done our best to make sure all website addresses in this book were active and appropriate when we went to press. However, the author and the publisher have no control over and assume no liability for the material available on those websites or on any websites they may link to. Any comments or suggestions can be sent by e-mail to customerservice@enslow.com.

Photo Credits: Cover, p. 1 spiber.de/Shutterstock.com; throughout book, mashuk/DigitalVision Vectors/Getty Images (tree background); Kathy Konkle/DigitalVision Vectors/Getty Images (tree & deer graphics); ulimi/DigitalVision Vectors/Getty Images (leaf graphics); paci77/DigitalVision Vectors/Getty Images (leaves); p. 4 Inga Nielsen/Shutterstock.com; p. 6 Designua/Shutterstock.com; p. 7 iStock.com/David Sucsy; p. 10 iStock.com/Sean Pavone; p. 11 Aleksey Stemmer/Shutterstock.com; p. 12 iStock.com/Dieter Meyrl; p. 13 Jim Cumming/Moment/Getty Images; p. 15 Shooty Photography/Shutterstock.com; p. 17 Steven Xiong/EyeEm/Getty Images; p. 19 Thomas Trutschel/Photothek/Getty Images; p. 21 Debbie Steinhausser/Shutterstock.com; p. 23 arbit/Shutterstock.com (forest), Tomacco/DigitalVision Vectors/Getty Images (animals).